OF FABLES

THE (NEARLY) GREAT ESCAPE

D1495071

FABLES OF

THE (NEARLY) GREAT ESCAPE

JACK OF FABLES
created by
BILL WILLINGHAM

WRITERS
BILL **Willingham**
MATTHEW **Sturges**

PENCILLER
TONY **Akins**

INKER
ANDREW **Pepoy**

COLORIST
DANIEL **VOZZO**

LETTERER
TODD **KLEIN**

ORIGINAL SERIES COVERS
JAMES **JEAN**

Cover illustration and logo by James Jean.

Publication design by Brainchild Studios/NYC.

JACK OF FABLES: THE (NEARLY) GREAT ESCAPE

Published by DC Comics. Cover, compilation and character sketches copyright © 2007 DC Comics. All Rights Reserved.

Originally published in single magazine form as JACK OF FABLES 1-5. Copyright © 2006, 2007 Bill Willingham and DC Comics. All Rights Reserved.
All characters, their distinctive likenesses and related elements featured in this publication are trademarks of Bill Willingham. VERTIGO is a trade-
mark of DC Comics. The stories, characters and incidents featured in this publication are entirely fictional. DC Comics does not read or accept
unsolicited submissions of ideas, stories or artwork.

DC Comics, 1700 Broadway, New York, NY 10019

A Warner Bros. Entertainment Company.

Printed in Canada. First Printing.

ISBN: 1-4012-1222-0

ISBN 13: 978-1-4012-1222-3

TABLE OF CONTENTS

LIFE IS A GIANT, COAGULATED BOWL OF SUCK.

HERE I AM, OUT ON THE ROAD, WITH A BRIEFCASE FULL OF MONEY AND NOWHERE IN PARTICULAR TO GO.

WHAT'S THAT YOU SAY? MOST MEN WOULD *LOVE* TO BE IN MY SITUATION? YOUNG, FIT, ACHINGLY HANDSOME AND FREE TO WANDER AS I WILL, UN-ENCUMBERED BY ANY OBLIGATION?

NO JOB, AND NO FAMILY OR HOME OR FRIENDS TO CLAW, SCRATCH, WHINE OR WEASEL FOR THEIR IMAGINED SHARE OF MY BIG BAG OF *CASH?*

YEAH, PUT IT THAT WAY AND IT DOESN'T SOUND SO BAD.

BUT WHAT IF, UP UNTIL JUST TWO DAYS AGO, YOU WERE MUCH, *MUCH* BETTER OFF?

INTRIGUED? YEAH, I THOUGHT YOU MIGHT BE. WHAT THE HELL-- SIT BACK, RELAX, SHUT UP FOR TEN MINUTES, AND I'LL TELL YOU MY TALE OF GLORY AND WOE.

THE LONG HARD FALL OF HOLLYWOOD JACK

'n which our hero is offered a ride, turns it down, takes it anyway, and ends up finding many new Fables, including one we've already met before.

✠ ☆ ✠ ☆ ✠ ☆ ✠ ☆ ✠ ☆ ✠ ☆ ✠ ☆ ✠ ☆ ✠ ☆ ✠ ☆ ✠ ☆ ✠ ☆ ✠ ☆ ✠ ☆ ✠ ☆ ✠

HAVE A DRINK, **ASSHOLE!**

BEGINNING TO CATCH ON? WHEN ONE HAD BILLIONS, A SINGLE BRIEFCASE FULL OF MONEY (THAT DOESN'T ADD UP TO MUCH MORE THAN A MILLION) IS THE VERY DEFINITION OF SUCKITUDE.

THINGS WENT BAD WHEN A TRAITOROUS LILLIPUTIAN THUG NAMED JILL RATTED ME OUT TO THE FABLETOWN AUTHORITIES.

HE'S OUT HERE IN **HOLLYWOOD** GOING UNDER THE NAME OF JOHN TRICK!

IF ONE OF YOU **NEEDLE-DICKS** GOT YOUR HEAD OUT OF YOUR **ASS** LONG ENOUGH TO WANDER INTO ANY MUNDY MOVIE HOUSE, YOU'D HAVE BEEN ABLE TO FIGURE THIS OUT ON YOUR OWN!

Nimble

THEY SENT THEIR NEW SHERIFF TO LOWER THE HAMMER ON ME.

GET LOST, JACK-- **LITERALLY.** YOU'VE BROKEN EVERY IMPORTANT FABLE LAW.

WE **OWN** YOUR STUDIOS NOW.

I'LL LET YOU TAKE AS MUCH CASH AS YOU CAN FIT INTO THIS BRIEFCASE, BUT THAT'S IT.

NO FAIR! THAT'S NOT A **FRACTION** OF MY ASSETS!

OUR ASSETS, JACK. YOU ORIGINALLY STOLE IT FROM US, AND WE'RE TAKING IT BACK.

AND NEVER SHOW YOUR FACE IN FABLETOWN AGAIN, OR WE'LL IMPLEMENT THE DEATH PENALTY **FIRST** AND WORRY ABOUT YOUR TRIAL **LATER.**

YOU USED TO BE A NICE GUY, BEAST. BUT GIVE YOU A LITTLE POWER AND OH, HOW THE **REAL** ASSHOLE EMERGES.

OKAY, MAYBE I BETTER EXPLAIN ALL THE MENTIONS OF "FABLES" FOR YOU READERS WHO ARE A BIT SLOW ON THE UPTAKE.

I'M A FABLE--WHICH MEANS I'M NOT QUITE HUMAN, AND NOT ORIGINALLY FROM *THIS* WORLD.

YOU KNOW SOME OF US--AT LEAST YOU *THINK* YOU KNOW US.

SNOW WHITE.

MR. MAYOR, TO HAVE ANY CHANCE OF MAKING OUR *BUDGET* THIS YEAR, WE'RE GOING TO HAVE TO RAISE *RENTS* IN THE WOODLAND ACROSS THE BOARD.

Ms. White

WE'RE THE LEGENDARY PEOPLE YOU'VE READ ABOUT IN YOUR STORYBOOKS.

PRINCE CHARMING.

OF COURSE I'D LIKE TO INVITE YOU *HOME* WITH ME--

--BUT I JUST MET YOU FIVE *MINUTES* AGO.

YOU KNOW EVERYTHING YOU NEED TO KNOW ABOUT ME. I'M YOUR HANDSOME *PRINCE*, COME TO TAKE YOU AWAY FROM ALL THIS.

THE BIG BAD WOLF.

TOO MANY CANDLES ON *THIS* CAKE!

NO SOONER DO I MAKE MY DEMANDS OF THE UNIVERSE THAN A DARK VAN SLOWS DOWN TO TAKE A GANDER AT ME.

THIS IS NO DOUBT ANOTHER FUNCTION OF MY NEW POWERS AS THE MOST POPULAR FABLE IN THE MUNDY WORLD.

ABOUT *TIME*.

OKAY, THIS COULD BE INTERESTING.

GOING *OUR* WAY, COWBOY?

YOUNG LADY--

--I HAPPEN TO BE GOING *EXACTLY* WHEREVER IT IS *YOU'RE* GOING.

HUH?

WAIT A MINUTE! WHO ARE THESE STRANGE CUSTOMERS LURKING INSIDE THE VAN?

UH, ON SECOND THOUGHT, LADY, I'VE CHANGED MY MIND. I'VE DECIDED TO *WALK*.

NO, THAT WON'T DO AT ALL. WE'VE BEEN LOOKING FOR YOU FOR TOO LONG JUST TO LET YOU WALK AWAY NOW.

GET INSIDE, JACK HORNER.

THEY KNOW WHO I AM?

UH... OKAY, IF YOU *INSIST*.

I DO. GET *COMFORTABLE*, JACK. WE HAVE A LONG WAY TO GO.

KIDNAPPED? ME? THAT'S NOT THE WAY IT'S SUPPOSED TO WORK. I HESITATE TO ADMIT THAT I'VE BEEN THE *KIDNAPPER* ONCE OR TWICE IN MY LONG LIFE, BUT NEVER THE *KIDNAPPEE*.

SO, WHERE ARE WE GOING?

YOU'LL FIND OUT.

WHICH SIDE ARE YOU WORKING FOR?

EXCUSE ME?

WELL, IT'S OBVIOUS YOU EITHER WORK FOR FABLETOWN OR THE ADVERSARY. THEY'RE THE ONLY ONES IN THIS WIDE WORLD WHO'D KNOW MY *REAL* NAME.

IF IT'S FABLETOWN, TELL YOUR BOSS I'M REALLY *PISSED*.

SHERIFF BEAST *PROMISED* ME HE'D LET ME GO IF I STAY OUT OF SIGHT. DID THE SHIT-BIRD SUDDENLY CHANGE HIS MIND?

AND SINCE WHEN DO FABLES EMPLOY SUCH CRUDE *STRONG-ARM* TACTICS AGAINST EACH OTHER?

WHO SAYS WE'RE *FABLES*, JACK?

SO YOU'RE MORE OF THE *ADVERSARY'S* THUGS? DON'T YOU GUYS CALL YOURSELVES FABLES TOO? I THOUGHT THAT WAS SORT OF UNIVERSAL.

I'M SURE IT IS. BUT YOU MAY NEED TO THINK OUTSIDE THE *BOX* HERE, JACK.

IT'S A BIGGER, BADDER AND STRANGER WORLD THAN YOU MIGHT SUSPECT.

AREN'T *YOU* JUST LITTLE MISS CRYPTIC?

WELL, YOU HAVE *FUN* WITH THAT. ENJOY THE REST OF THE DRIVE ON YOUR OWN.

WHAM!

DID THESE MORONS SERIOUSLY THINK ANY FLIMSY MUNDY *DOOR* COULD HOLD ME? I'M JACK HORNER IN THE FULL FLUSH OF MY FABLE POWER!

18

NO ONE'S FOLLOWING. I THINK WE'RE CLEAR.

SO HE'S *DEAD*, RIGHT?

NOT SO MUCH, ACTUALLY. HE'S EVEN GOT A BIT OF A PULSE.

JEEZ, SO THE BOSS *WASN'T* KIDDING ABOUT THIS GUY.

APPARENTLY NOT.

OW! SON OF A *BITCH!*

HE'S FINALLY WAKING UP.

OKAY, SO IN RETROSPECT THAT *WASN'T* THE GREATEST PLAN I'VE EVER COME UP WITH.

OW. AND AGAIN I SAY *OW!*

HOW LONG WAS I OUT?

NEARLY TWO DAYS.

WELL, HOW DO YOU LIKE *THAT?* PRETTY COOL, HUH?

SNIK

SNIK

I WOULDN'T GET *TOO* COCKY JUST YET, JACK. WE'RE EXPERTS IN THE CAPTURE AND IMPRISONMENT OF FABLES.

WE'LL HAVE NO PROBLEM BREAKING YOU AGAIN IF YOU MISBEHAVE.

Private Road, No Trespassing

'Violators will' be prosecuted to the full extent of the law.

WE'RE ALMOST AT THE PERIMETER. I'LL RADIO AHEAD TO THE MAIN GATE.

MAIN LIBRARY, THIS IS BOOK RETURN ONE, REQUESTING PERIMETER CLEARANCE.

OH, PLEASE. YOU DON'T EXPECT TO KEEP ME LOCKED IN HERE WITH ONE TEENY LITTLE *FENCE*, DO YOU?

NO, NOT AT ALL.

BOOK RETURN ONE, YOU'RE CLEARED TO ENTER. WELCOME HOME.

THE FENCE IS TO KEEP THE *TIGERS* IN. THE TIGERS ARE FOR KEEPING *YOU* IN.

TIGERS?

OH, AND THE MOAT. AND THE GUARD TOWERS. AND THE GUARDS. AND A FEW *OTHER* NASTY SURPRISES. FACE IT, JACK, THIS IS YOUR NEW *HOME*, WHETHER YOU LIKE IT OR *NOT*.

22

LINDY, WILL YOU SIGN THE VAN BACK INTO THE MOTOR POOL AND RETURN THE BAGMEN TO STORAGE?

SAM?

OH, *SAM*, WILL YOU COME OVER HERE?

YES, MISS PAGE?

SAM, THIS IS *JACK,* OUR NEW GUEST. I HAVE TO RUN UP TO THE LIBRARY TO REPORT IN, SO WILL YOU SHOW JACK UP TO HIS COTTAGE?

I THINK HE'S AT THE ALDER.

AND SEE IF CHICKEN LAUNDRESS CAN BE PERSUADED TO ADVANCE HIM SOMETHING FROM THE CLOTHING COMMISSARY.

YES, MISS PAGE. COME THIS WAY, YOUNG FELLA.

DON'T TAKE THIS THE WRONG WAY, OLD-TIMER, BUT IF *YOU'RE* AN EXAMPLE OF THE CALIBER OF GUARDS AROUND HERE, I'LL BE GONE BY SUNDOWN.

OH, I'M NOT A GUARD. I'M A PRISONER, STUCK HERE JUST LIKE YOU. BUT I'M ONE OF THE TRUSTEES.

AND I'M A TOUCH MORE *SPRY* THAN I LOOK--WHEN I NEED TO BE.

YOU'RE A FABLE? I DON'T RECOGNIZE YOU.

I DON'T RIGHTLY *KNOW* IF I' A FABLE ANY MORE.

24

THEY DID SUCH A GOOD JOB OF *KILLING* MY STORY THAT NARY A SINGLE MUNDY REMEMBERS ME.

THAT'S WHAT *THEY* DO. THEY KEEP US HERE WHILE THEY MAKE EVERYONE OUT THERE FORGET OUR STORIES.

UNTIL WE'RE AS *MUNDANE* AS THE MUNDYS.

THAT WON'T HAPPEN TO *ME*, OLD FART. I WON'T BE HERE LONG ENOUGH.

YOU THINK SO *NOW*, BUT YOU'LL FIND OUT DIFFERENT, ONCE YOU HAVE YOUR WELCOME CHAT WITH MISTER REVISE.

WHO'S HE?

IN A NORMAL PRISON, HE'D BE CALLED OUR WARDEN. DON'T CALL HIM HAT, THOUGH. HE DON'T LIKE IT. OVER THE YEARS I'VE HEARD HIM CALLED BY *LOTS* OF ODD AND FANCY TITLES.

THE CUTTING MAN, WARLOCK'S BANE, THE UNMAKER AND THE MASTER LIBRARIAN, AMONG OTHERS I PROBABLY FORGOT.

AND HIS COHORTS CALL THEMSELVES SENIOR LIBRARIAN THIS, AND ASSISTANT LIBRARIAN THAT, AND SO ON. SOUNDS NICE AND GENTLE LIKE, BUT IT ALL TRANSLATES INTO *THUG.*

THEY'RE A *NASTY* BUNCH IF YOU RILE THEM.

WHAT ABOUT THE QUIET MEN IN THE HEAD-TO-TOE RAINCOATS?

THEY'RE THE WORST, AND DON'T *EVER* MAKE THE MISTAKE OF THINKING THEY'RE *MEN*.

THEY AIN'T. THEY'RE SOMETHING...ELSE. THINK TWICE BEFORE YOU CROSS ONE. YOU *WON'T* LIKE THE OUTCOME.

DON'T WORRY ABOUT *ME*, SAMMY. I CAN GIVE A GOOD ACCOUNTING OF MYSELF.

I'VE KILLED MORE GIANTS THAN YOU CAN *COUNT*. THESE GUYS DON'T LOOK SO TOUGH COMPARED TO THAT.

SUIT YOUR-SELF.

THIS HERE'S YOUR PLACE. YOU'LL FIND A ROBE IN THE CLOSET UNTIL I CAN GET SOME PROPER CLOTHES SENT UP. PROBABLY TOMORROW.

HEY, WAIT A MINUTE, GRANDPA. AREN'T YOU GOING TO LOCK ME *IN*?

NOPE. YOU CAN COME AND GO AS YOU PLEASE HERE, EXCEPT BE INSIDE BY DARK AND DON'T EVER CROSS THE STONE WALL SURROUNDING THE COMPOUND.

THE BAD THINGS GENERALLY STAY ON THE FAR SIDE OF THAT AS LONG AS WE BEHAVE OUR-SELVES.

PLEASURE MEETING YOU, JACK.

SO THIS IS IT, HUH? *THIS* IS WHERE I'M SUPPOSED TO LIVE OUT MY THEORETICALLY ENDLESS DAYS?

NOT BLOODY LIKELY.

I'M USED TO SLIGHTLY BETTER ACCOMMODATIONS.

WHAT'S THIS? THEY COULDN'T EVEN CLEAN *UP* AFTER THE LAST GUY?

LOOK AT THIS. SOMEONE'S BEEN EATING MY-- WHATEVER THE HELL THAT IS.

PORRIDGE?

AND SOMEONE'S BEEN SITTING IN MY CHAIR.

WELL, THEY BETTER NOT HAVE BEEN--

SOME- ONE'S BEEN SLEEPING IN MY *BED.*

In which our hero makes time and does time, two drunks fight in a bar, and an egg scrambles.

SUN SHINING BRIGHTLY THROUGH THE BEDROOM CURTAINS. BIRDS MERRILY CHIRPING, AND ALL THAT OTHER HAPPY MORNING *CRAP.* GIVE ME A BREAK.

OKAY, I'M NOT A MORNING PERSON. IT TAKES ME A WHILE TO GET MY MOTOR RUNNING. BUT I'M *STILL* BETTER THAN ANY OF YOU.

GO BACK AND READ THE FIRST SCENE IN THIS BOOK AGAIN, WHILE I SHAKE THE FUZZ OUT OF MY HEAD AND CLAW THE DRIED SLEEP CRUST OUT OF MY EYES.

:GRRRRRRRRR:

FINE. SUIT YOURSELF, BUT DON'T BLAME *ME* IF YOU SEE SOME THINGS YOU'D RATHER NOT.

OH CRAP.

YEAH, IT'S GOLDILOCKS.

GET *UP*, GOLDIE. IT'S DAYTIME. YOU *NEED* TO GO HOME.

HMMMM?

OH, GET THAT SHOCKED LOOK OFF YOUR FACE. JUST BECAUSE SHE'S AN INSANE KILLER DIDN'T MEAN I WASN'T GOING TO *SLEEP* WITH HER.

JACK? GOOD MORNING. HAND ME MY GLASSES.

LOOK AT HER. YOU WOULD'VE DONE IT TOO.

UNLESS YOU WANT TO *VIOLATE* ME AGAIN?

ERM, NO.

YOU *HAVE* TO GET OUT. I NEED MY MORNINGS ALONE. NO BREAKFAST. NO COFFEE. NO TOAST. JUST *GO*.

SURE SHE TRIED TO KILL SNOW WHITE--*TWICE*--AND THAT'S BAD. BUT SHE ALSO TRIED TO KILL BIGBY WOLF, AND THAT'S OKAY IN MY BOOK.

YOU DON'T WANT TO TALK ABOUT OLD TIMES?

YOU AND I DIDN'T *HAVE* ANY OLD TIMES.

SURE WE DID. WE WERE OPPRESSED MEMBERS OF THE FABLETOWN *PROLETARIAT* TOGETHER, EVEN IF I SPENT MOST OF MY TIME AT THE *GULAG* THEY CALLED THE FARM.

MOST OF THE FABLES HERE NEVER *SAW* FABLETOWN.

THEY WERE CAPTURED *CENTURIES* AGO AND HAVE LIVED HERE-- UTTERLY DIS-POSSESSED-- EVER SINCE.

THAT'S YOUR *FIRST* LIE OF THE DAY, GOLDIE. I TRAVELED *THROUGH* HERE CENTURIES AGO AND IT WAS UNTOUCHED WILDER-NESS.

OH SURE. THEY SAY THE ACTUAL **SETTLEMENT** HAS MOVED MANY TIMES, BUT IT'S ALWAYS BASICALLY THE SAME PLACE.

OKAY, FINE. IT'S **OBVIOUS** YOU'RE NOT GOING TO VAMOOSE UNTIL YOU'VE HAD YOUR MORNING-AFTER CHAT. SO TELL ME HOW YOU ENDED UP HERE, ALIVE AND WELL.

THE **SHORT** VERSION WILL DO JUST FINE. SNOW TOLD US YOU WERE DEAD.

I WAS PRETTY BAD OFF--**THAT'S** FOR SURE. BUT I'M ONE OF THE FEW FABLES EVERYONE IN THIS OPPRESSIVE WHITE MALE-DOMINATED CULTURAL HEGEMONY KNOWS BY NAME.

"SO I CAN'T BE KILLED EASILY.

"SURE, THE AX IN THE HEAD WAS BAD.

"AND THE TUMBLE DOWN A CLIFF WAS CERTAINLY NO PICNIC.

"AND GETTING RUN OVER BY THAT LOGGING TRUCK NEARLY **FINISHED** ME."

"BUT GETTING DUMPED FACE DOWN IN A RIVER? THAT WAS THE WORST OF ALL.

"BY THAT TIME I WAS TOO SEVERELY WOUNDED TO HAVE ENOUGH CONTROL OVER MY BODY TO GET MY HEAD ABOVE WATER."

SO I FLOATED DOWNSTREAM, *DROWNING* ALL THE WAY, BUT NEVER QUITE ABLE TO FINISH DYING.

THAT'S A GOOD GIRL. FINISH DRESSING WHILE YOU TALK. HERE'RE YOUR SHOES.

"IT WAS THE MOST AGONIZING FORM OF TORTURE IMAGINABLE AND IT LASTED FOR DAYS--*WEEKS* PROBABLY.

"I BEGGED GODDESS, THE UNIVERSE, OR *ANY* POWER AT ALL TO KILL ME.

"NO SUCH LUCK.

PUGET SOUND

"THAT STREAM FED INTO A LARGER RIVER, AND THAT FLUSHED INTO THE PACIFIC OCEAN."

"BY THEN I WAS STARTING TO RECOVER, BUT THE FISH WERE GETTING AT ME. SO THEN THE QUESTION WAS, COULD I *HEAL* FASTER THAN THEY WERE *EATING* ME?

"MR. REVISE EVENTUALLY FOUND ME AND FISHED ME OUT.

"HE HAS *WAYS* OF FINDING US WHEN HE WANTS TO."

LET ME TELL YOU SOMETHING, JACKIE BOY. SOMEDAY EVERYONE WHO DEFIED ME WILL SUFFER. THE WAY *I* SUFFERED. SNOW. AND BIGBY. AND--

OKAY, TIME TO LOSE *PSYCHO* GIRL.

NICE STORY, GOLDIE. I *REALLY* LIKE THE PART WHERE YOU FINALLY STOPPED TALKING. LET'S DO THIS AGAIN SOON.

YEAH, DROP BY AGAIN-- AT LEAST A *MONTH* AFTER I'M GONE.

REMEMBER, JACK, I AM THE UNSILENCED *VOICE* OF THE OPPRESSED MASSES, AND WE HAVE POWER YOU CAN'T *IMAGINE!*

OKEY DOKE. SORRY YOU COULDN'T STAY.

37

38

DING DONG
The U'Mundy

HELLO?

ANYBODY HOME?

DOWN HERE! BASE-MENT!

FWOOOZ!

The U'Mundy

C'MON, YOU LITTLE BASTARD.

PLACK! PLACK!

UM, EXCUSE ME, I'M LOOKING FOR A JACK HORNER?

YOU FOUND ONE. GOOD FOR YOU.

POWER UP! — OOH! UN-MUNDY!

YES, UH. I'M SUPPOSED TO TAKE YOU TO YOUR UM MEETING WITH MISTER REVISE.

SORRY, NOW'S NOT A GOOD--AW, MAN! NOW LOOK WHAT YOU MADE ME DO!

PLACK! PLACK!

OUCH! THAT'S GOTTA HURT!

41

AND I THOUGHT *FABLE-TOWN* WAS AN ODD PLACE.

GARY.

WHAT?

THAT'S WHAT I ALWAYS HOPED PEOPLE WOULD CALL ME.

THAT, OR LANCE.

YEP. OKAY.

SO TELL ME, LITTLE MAN, IS THE BOOZE IN THIS BAR FREE? JUST LIKE THE FOOD AND CLOTHES AND ALL THAT?

UHM, YES, BUT YOU'RE ALREADY *AWFULLY* LATE FOR YOUR APPOINTMENT, AND I DON'T THINK IT WOULD BE WISE TO--

YOUR BOSS SOUNDS LIKE A REASONABLE GUY. H WON'T MIND IF WE HAV A DRINK OR THREE FIRST. COME ON IN, LITTLE BUDDY.

42

IT'S NOT EVEN LUNCHTIME! WHO DRINKS SO *EARLY* IN THE DAY?

THOSE OF US WHO CAN'T ABIDE PROCRASTINATION.

BARTENDER! SET ME UP WITH A SHOT AND A BEER!

AH, A GENTLEMAN OF DISCRIMINATING TASTE!

YOU TOO, GARY. *YOU'RE* GOING TO START IN NOW?

WE CAN DRINK *ANYTIME* WE WANT TO!

SO *MIND* YOUR OWN BEESWAX!

SORRY, MR. BUNYAN, SIR! BEG YOUR PARDON!

HEY, BIG FELLA!

LEAVE THE POOR LITTLE DUDE ALONE! HE WASN'T EVEN *TALKING* TO YOU!

AND I WASN'T TALKING TO *YOU*, STRANGER. SO BUTT RIGHT-THE-FUCK *OUT* BEFORE I STOMP YOU *FLAT*.

HARDER THAN IT LOOKS, TALL, DARK AND *TUBBY*.

I'M NOT ABOUT TO BE SCARED OF A GUY WHO SPENDS *FAR* TOO MUCH OF HIS TIME ALONE IN THE WOODS WITH A BLUE COW.

SHE'S *NOT* A COW.

43

YOU ARE JACK HORNER. PSEUDONYMS INCLUDE JACK OF THE TALES, JACK B. NIMBLE, JOHN TRICK, JACK THE GIANT-KILLER. AM I LEAVING ANY OUT?

JACK FROST. BUT THAT WAS A DIFFERENT COUNTRY, AND THE SOLDIERS ARE ALL FROZEN.

THIS HAS BEEN FUN, BUT I'VE *GOT* TO GET GOING. I--

THE CHAIR YOU'RE SITTING IN DATES TO FOURTEENTH-CENTURY FRANCE. IT WAS USED BY THE PAPAL INQUISITION TO INTERROGATE CATHARS.

LIKE THOSE INQUISITORS, I *LOATHE* SUCH PARLOR TRICKS. BUT ALSO LIKE THEM, I BELIEVE THEY HAVE THEIR USES.

HE'S IN THERE WITH REVISE NOW? THE NEW GUY?

YES. HE'S BEEN IN THERE FOR A LITTLE WHILE NOW.

SAM, WHAT'S HE LIKE? IS HE CUTE?

HOW SHOULD I KNOW?

IS HE REALLY, YOU KNOW, THE JACK? OF THE TALES?

I SUPPOSE HE IS. AND HE'S QUITE A SPECIMEN, I CAN TELL YOU. BUT DON'T YOU GO GETTING ANY IDEAS THAT HE'S SOME KIND OF SAVIOR, MARY MARY. A FELLOW LIKE HIM IS APT TO GET FOLKS HURT.

WELL, I DISAGREE.

YOU COULD HARDLY DO OTHERWISE, CHILD.

DO YOU KNOW WHAT MY JOB IS, DEAR BOY? MY **CALLING?**

SEAMSTRESS? GAY BLADE? WACKY BARBER?

MY **JOB** IS TO EMASCULATE YOU, JACK.

YOU-- DO **WHAT**, NOW?

NOT LITERALLY, THOUGH THAT WOULD CERTAINLY BE ENJOYABLE IN YOUR CASE. WITH THE DULL SHEARS OF TIME AND DISTANCE I WILL SNIP AWAY AT YOUR VIRILITY, YOUR **POWER.** YOUR VERY ESSENCE.

"DO YOU EVEN REMEMBER ANY-MORE, JACK?"

"HOW MUCH MORE SENSUAL IT USED TO BE? HOW VIOLENT? HOW CONCUPISCENT?"

"MY JOB IS TO **NEUTER** YOU; TO TAKE AWAY ALL IN YOU THAT IS POTENT AND FEARSOME.

"ALL THAT IS MEMORABLE AND DISTINCT."

AND YOU'VE SINGLED ME OUT **WHY**, EXACTLY?

WHY?

WHY? DEAR BOY, WHEN I FIRST CAME TO THIS WORLD IT WAS *FILTHY* WITH MAGIC. WITCHES, ANGELS, DEVILS, PAGAN GODS--EVERY-WHERE.

WE NEARLY HAD THIS WORLD COMPLETELY FREE FROM THE PESTILENCE OF MAGIC WHEN *YOUR* KIND ARRIVED, POURING THROUGH THE GATES LIKE RATS FROM A SINKING SHIP.

I'VE STOPPED MUCH OF THE DECAY. BUT THANKS TO YOUR HOLLYWOOD STUNT, YOU'VE THREATENED TO UNDO *EVERYTHING* I'VE ACCOMPLISHED.

AND I'LL *KILL* YOU FOR IT.

KILL ME? I DON'T THINK SO.

LISTEN UP, FOUR-EYES. I'M *JACK* OF THE GODDAMN TALES--THE STAR OF ANY STORY I'M IN. WHEREAS YOU'RE NOTHING BUT A TWO-BIT HOOD FROM CENTRAL CASTING.

QUIET!

NO ONE HAS *EVER* ESCAPED ME.

RESIGN YOURSELF TO THE FACT THAT YOU'RE HERE FOR LIFE.

NOW GET *OUT* OF MY OFFICE.

50

NEXT: WE FIND OUT WHAT PRISON LIFE DOES TO NICE GIRLS, I BREAK A FEW MORE HEARTS, COMPOSE AN OPERA, SOLVE THE BRAZILIAN DEBT CRISIS AND WHIP THE GRIM REAPER HIMSELF AT ARM WRESTLING. ONLY A *FOOL* WOULD MISS IT.

THEN THERE'S THE TIGERS THAT PATROL AT NIGHT, JUST INSIDE THE OUTER FENCE LINE, AND THE *BAG MEN*, WHO'RE LET OUT ANYTIME THERE'S AN ESCAPE ATTEMPT.

I DON'T WANT TO TANGLE WITH ANY *TIGERS*, BUT THOSE BAG MEN DON'T SEEM SO TOUGH.

THEY ARE, THOUGH, JACK. YO[U] DON'T *EVER* WANT T[O] MESS WITH ONE OF THEM.

THANKS FOR THE ORGANIZA-TIONAL *TUTORIAL*, SAM.

ARE THE BAG MEN THOSE GUYS IN BLACK, WITH GOGGLES AND SHIT? THERE WERE TWO OF THEM IN THE VAN WHEN THEY NABBED ME.

OKAY, ONE OTHER THING THAT BUGS ME ABOUT THIS PLACE. THERE'S LOTS OF *BIRD* TYPE FABLES IMPRISONED HERE.

WHY DON'T THEY ALL JUST FLY AWAY?

NOT POSSIBLE, MR. HORNER. EACH GUARD TOWER HAS A CAGE WITH A DOUBLING ROOK IN IT.

IF YOU TRY TO FLY AWAY, THE NEAREST TOWER GUARD *ALWAYS* KNOWS IT AND RELEASES HIS ROOK.

YOU DON'T KNOW JACK

In which plot[s] are plotted, schemes are schemed, and [a] great escape i[s] planned.

HEY'RE SCARY.

AND NOT REALLY MEN, I FEAR.

BASICALLY THEY'LL KICK YOUR ASS, JACK--WHICH, COME TO THINK OF IT, WOULDN'T BE THE *WORST* THING IN THE WORLD.

SO, FORGET WHAT WE SAID. GO AHEAD AND PICK A FIGHT WITH ONE'A THEM BAGGY DUDES.

"THEN YOU WANT TO GROUND YOURSELF *IMMEDIATELY*, 'CAUSE ANYTHING IN THE SKY IS--WELL, IT GETS REAL BAD UP THERE."

OKAY, THAT'S SUFFICIENTLY *CRYPTIC*. WHAT IS IT ABOUT FABLES THAT WE CAN'T EVER GIVE STRAIGHT, SIMPLE *ANSWERS* TO STRAIGHT, SIMPLE *QUESTIONS*?

ASK A FABLE A QUESTION AND YOU GET A SPOOKY STORY.

BUT, SPEAKING OF *ACTUAL* THREATS, LIKE GUARD TOWERS-- HOW MANY ARE THERE?

SIXTEEN-- SPACED PRETTY REGULAR AROUND THE FENCE LINE.

AND HOW MANY TIGERS?

I WAS NEVER INSPIRED TO TRY TO COUNT THEM.

OKAY, KIDS, WE'VE BEEN HERE LONG ENOUGH FOR ONE MEETING.

BEST BREAK IT UP BEFORE ANY OF THE SCREWS BEGIN TO WONDER WHERE WE ARE.

SAM WILL TELL YOU *WHERE* AND *WHEN* WE MEET AGAIN.

DON'T ALL LEAVE AT ONCE AND DON'T *ANYONE* TALK ABOUT THIS OUTSIDE, NOT EVEN TO EACH OTHER.

YES, OPERATIONAL SECURITY IS *ESSENTIAL.*

SAM, YOU'LL BURN THAT CHART AFTER WE LEAVE?

YEP.

HOLD ON, EGG BOY, AND MA GOOSE. I NEED TO TALK TO YOU TWO.

HERE'S THE DEAL, GUYS. YOU TWO DON'T *LOOK* VERY HUMAN. EVEN IF YOU GET AWAY IN THE BIG BREAKOUT--

--HOW DO YOU THINK YOU'RE GOING TO FIT INTO THE MUNDY WORLD OUT THERE?

YOU KNOW, I USED TO BE A HUMAN, AS HUMAN AS ONE CAN BE.

BUT ALL THE MUNDYS CONFUSED MY NAME AND MADE A REAL GOOSE OUT OF ME.

UH...YEAH... THAT WAS A FASCINATING STORY, LADY. BUT I'M AFRAID YOU *CAN'T* GO WITH US.

YOU NEITHER, HUMPTY DUMPTY.

THAT'S TOO BAD.

I GOT SOMETHING YOU'LL BE *VERY* INTERESTED IN, JACK OF THE TALES. SOMETHING I SQUIRRELED AWAY BEFORE THE BAGMEN TOOK ME.

OH YEAH? LIKE *WHAT?*

JUST THE KEY TO A KING'S RANSOM, IS ALL.

YOU'RE NOT SHITTING ME, ARE YOU, FATTY?

YOU SPRING ME, YOU CAN SEE FOR YOURSELF.

OKAY, EGG BOY'S *BACK* IN THE ESCAPE.

WHAT ABOUT YOU, GOOSE MAMA? CAN YOU LAY GIANT GOLDEN EGGS OR SOMETHING?

NO, I'M SORRY, BUT NO EGGS OF GOLD.

MY *ONLY* TREASURES ARE IN STORIES TOLD.

SORRY, THEN. YOU'RE OUT.

JACK AND JILL WENT UP THE HOLLYWOOD HILLS, TO FETCH A PAIL OF GLITTER...

...BUT JACK FELL DOWN AND BROKE HIS CROWN, AND LANDED WITH US IN THE SHITTER.

HEY, FELLA, WHAT'S THAT SUPPOSED TO MEAN? AND JUST WHO THE HELL ARE *YOU* ANYWAY?

EVERYONE CALLS ME WICKED JOHN, BUT THEY'RE WRONG. I'M AS NICE AS I NEED TO BE.

YOU LOOK FAMILIAR.

YOU FINALLY NOTICED? CLEVER BOY. IT ONLY TOOK YOU TWO WEEKS.

HAVE WE MET?

OH, I SEE YOU HAVEN'T ACTUALLY FIGURED ANYTHING OUT AT ALL. NO, JACK, WE'VE NEVER MET PER SE.

NOW LISTEN HERE, BUDDY! I DON'T KNOW WHY YOU'VE GOT SUCH A NUT AGAINST ME, BUT WHY DON'T YOU AND ME STEP OUT BEHIND THE--

SURE, I'D LOVE TO BEAT THE SHIT OUT OF YOU, JACK, BUT NOT RIGHT NOW.

SHHHHHH. NON-ESCAPE-CONSPIRACY PRISONER APPROACHING.

WHY HELLO, ALICE.

HELLO, JOHN.

IT'S SUCH A PRETTY DAY, ALICE. WOULD YOU LIKE TO TAKE A STROLL DOWN BY THE--

GOODBYE, JOHN.

ALL THE YOUNG GIRLS LOVE ALICE. TENDER YOUNG ALICE THEY SAY...

DO ME THE COURTESY OF *DYING* SOON, JOHN.

I SWEAR THAT GIRL *ADORES* ME.

THERE YOU ARE, JACK. SHALL WE GO TO ONE OF THE CAFÉS FOR LUNCH?

HOW ABOUT *THE WILLOW LEAF?* THEY HAVE GOOD SOUPS.

GOLDILOCKS, YOU CAN'T KEEP HANGING ALL OVER ME IN PUBLIC LIKE THIS.

WHAT?

HEY, DON'T GET ME WRONG, BABE. I LIKE BOINKING YOU EVERY NIGHT, BUT WE *AREN'T* A COUPLE.

BUT--? JACK, YOU CAN BE SUCH A COMPLETE--

AND I DON'T HAVE TIME FOR LUNCH JUST NOW. I HAVE AN APPOINTMENT UP ON ADMINISTRATION HILL.

GO GET YOUR SOUP, AND *THEN* YOU CAN HEAD BACK TO YOUR COTTAGE, GET NAKED, AND WAIT FOR ME--IF YOU WANT.

JACKASS!

HOW THE *HELL* DID YOU GET IN HERE?

FILL IT UP.

WHAT?

WHEN YOU STUFFED ME IN THE BACK OF YOUR A-TEAM VAN, THIS *CASE* CONTAINED *EXACTLY* ONE MILLION, ONE HUNDRED AND FORTY-TWO THOUSAND DOLLARS.

I WANT IT ALL BACK. *EVERY* PENNY.

OKAY, JACK. DISREGARDING THE FACT THAT THERE'S NO WAY IT'S GOING TO HAPPEN, WHAT COULD YOU *POSSIBLY* NEED THE MONEY FOR IN THE FIRST PLACE?

EVERYTHING AROUND HERE IS *FREE* FOR RESIDENTS-- FOOD, CLOTHING, BOOZE, YOU NAME IT.

THAT'S SWEET, BUT I DON'T PLAN TO *BE* HERE VERY LONG. SO YOU CAN SEE MY PROBLEM.

I SEE YOUR PROBLEM, JACK OF THE TALES. BUT I'M NOT SURE **YOU** DO.

I IMAGINE YOU'RE USED TO TREATING LIFE AS IF IT'S ALL A BIG GAME. BUT THIS IS DIFFERENT.

WE CAN HURT YOU. MY SISTERS AND I **EAT** FAIRY TALES LIKE YOU FOR BREAKFAST.

WE HAVE WAYS OF CAUSING PAIN TO FABLEKIND THAT YOU'VE NEVER EVEN **DREAMED** OF.

SO I SUGGEST YOU TAKE YOUR CASE AND GET OUT OF MY OFFICE RIGHT **NOW**, BEFORE I DECIDE TO MAKE AN EXAMPLE OF YOU.

ARE YOU FLIRTING WITH ME?

GET OUT!

THAT ONE GETS UNDER YOUR *SKIN*, DOESN'T HE, PRIS?

SHUT UP.

THAT WAS *HOT*.

HE'S A SHOW-OFF. TALKS BIG. IRRITATING AS HELL. *YOUR* TYPE.

BUT IS HE ALL BARK AND NO BITE? I DON'T *THINK* SO.

MEANING?

HE'S PLANNING SOMETHING. IT'S ALL *OVER* THE PLACE. NONE OF MY SNITCHES HAVE BEEN INVITED TO JOIN, BUT I'M PRETTY SURE HE'S PUTTING TOGETHER AN OLD-FASHIONED JAILBREAK.

ROBIN-- YOU THINK WE SHOULD TELL REVISE?

DOES THE POPE SHIT IN THE WOODS?

LISTEN, WITH YOUR TWENTY-CAR PILEUP ON THE INTER-STATE AND MY NEARLY LOSING A THREE-HUNDRED-POUND EGG OVER THE FENCE, I THINK WE COULD *BOTH* USE SOME BROWNIE POINTS.

HEAD LIBRARIAN

ENTER.

...SO WE THOUGHT IT WISE TO BRING IT TO YOUR ATTENTION.

I WAS WONDERING WHEN ONE OF YOU WOULD PUT IT TOGETHER. I'VE KNOWN ABOUT IT FOR *DAYS*.

I'M DISAPPOINTED IN YOU.

WE ONLY STARTED PICKING UP SIGNS YESTERDAY ON OUR SURVEILLANCE. WHERE ARE YOU GETTING YOUR INFORMATION?

I HAVE AN OPERATIVE AMONG THE CONSPIRATORS. ONE OF MY *PRIVATE* AGENTS.

YOU CAN'T KEEP THESE THINGS FROM ME, BOSS. I NEED TO KNOW *WHO'S* ON OUR SIDE SO I CAN DO MY JOB.

DO YOU PRESUME TO TELL ME *MY* BUSINESS, GIRL? IF THERE IS INFORMATION *I* DEEM YOU WORTHY OF KNOWING, YOU WILL *KNOW* IT.

"THE OPERATIVE'S IDENTITY IS *NOT* YOUR CONCERN."

HEY, THERE. WHAT ARE YOU DOING, JACK?

OH, HI, SAM. I'M CLIMBING THIS TREE.

YOU'RE NOT SUPPOSED TO BE *IN* THERE, SONNY BOY. THAT'S WHY THERE'S A FENCE AROUND IT.

YEAH, BUT I WANT TO GET A LOOK AT AS MANY GUARD TOWERS AS I CAN SEE AT ONCE--

--SO I CAN SPY ANY BLIND SPOTS IN THEIR PLACEMENT. BUT WITHOUT ACTUALLY *WALKING* THE TOWER LINE AND DRAWING ATTENTION TO MYSELF.

SO, UP I CLIMB.

I DON'T THINK THAT'S A GOOD IDEA, JACK. THIS HERE'S AN OLD TREE, AND SOME OF THE BRANCHES AREN'T AS *SPRY* AS THEY USED TO BE.

WHAT?

CRACK!

SAM, I HAVE TO TELL YOU SOMETHING.

SWEET JESUS, BOY!

LISTEN, SAM.

THIS REALLY, REALLY HURTS. AND I MAY START TO CRY JUST A LITTLE BIT HERE IN A SECOND.

IF THAT HAPPENS--AND I'M ONLY SAYING IT *MIGHT*-- I JUST WANT YOU TO KNOW--

--THAT IF YOU TELL ANYONE ABOUT IT, I *WILL* KILL YOU.

Sam

WHY DON'T I SEE ABOUT GETTING YOU DOWN FROM THERE?

THAT'D BE SWELL.

I NEED ONE OF YOU BOYS TO RUN DOWN THE HILL AND FETCH THE FALLACY. *QUICK* NOW!

WANNA RACE?

HOW DO YOU FEEL, SON?

LIKE I JUST GOT *IMPALED* ON A FENCE. YOU?

GREAT WORK, FENCE. TOP DRAWER.

IF YOU CAN WALK, WE'D *BEST* BE MOVING ALONG. NO NEED TO ATTRACT ANY MORE NOTICE THAN WE ALREADY HAVE.

I PROBABLY SHOULDN'T TELL YOU THIS, BECAUSE YOU'RE *NOT* A VERY NICE PERSON, AND I COULD GET IN TROUBLE.

BUT I WANT TO *HELP* YOU AND SAM.

OKAY, I'M LISTENING.

YOU'RE CONCERNED ABOUT AN AIR ESCAPE. I HAD AN IDEA...

HOW DID *YOU*--?

DON'T WORRY ABOUT THAT.

GO TO BUILDING SIXTEEN. THE GIRLS THERE ARE WILLING TO HELP YOU. WHEN THE TIME COMES, I'LL LET THEM OUT.

HELLO, UM, LADIES.

OH, HOW I'VE DREAMED OF THIS MOMENT! JACK! JACK! MY HERO!

OF *COURSE* YOU REMEMBER MUSTARDSEED. AND PEASEBLOSSOM AND MOTH ARE RIGHT NEXT DOOR!

WHO'S *THIS* THEN, COBWEB-PET? OLD BOY-FRIEND?

OOH, YEAH! IF I FANCIED *LADS*, I MIGHT HAVE A GO AT HIM MYSELF!

NEVER YOU MIND, YOU COTTINGLEY DYKES. JACK'S A SAVIOR, HE IS. LIBERATED OUR PEOPLE FROM THE EVIL BOGGART NASTYFINGERS.

ASKED *NOTHING* IN RETURN.

MY HERO!

ALL WILL HOWL. ALL WILL BLEED. THE DOOR-KNOB TURNS IN THE TWILIGHT. PAIN! THEN...THE EMPTINESS.

I, UH-- YEAH?

WOULD YOU MIND FETCHING ME A CIGGIE, LOVE? THERE'S A LAD.

WELL, I'VE BEEN CALLED WORSE. IF YOU WANT TO CALL ME YOUR SAVIOR, I CAN *HARDLY* ARGUE.

OH, FAIRIES MOST FLEET AND MOST FOUL! PREPARE TO TASTE MY WILL AND MY WICK YET AGAIN!

I'LL HAVE THE LOT OF *YOU* FOR MY LOVES AND FOR MY LUNCH!

WHEN DID I EVER SAVE A BUNCH OF FAERIES?

SO THEN I WAS GOING TO SAY, "DROP YOUR SWORDS, YOU VARLETS!"

AND SHE'D HAVE SAID, "OH, JACK!"

PLEASE, *NO!*

SOMEBODY *HELP* US!

AND I'D HAVE TURNED TO THOSE BASTARDS--BRANDISHING MY *SWORD*--AND SAID...

...NOBODY THREATENS MY MAIDENS FAIR AND LIVES TO TELL THE TALE!

⸝ULK!⸝

WHO *WAS* THAT HANDSOME GIANT?

WHA--?

IT'S MIDNIGHT. WE NEED TO MEET THE OTHERS IN *FIFTEEN* MINUTES.

WE'RE SCHEDULED FOR A WALK-THROUGH OF NEXT WEEK'S ESCAPE PLAN, REMEMBER?

OH YEAH, I'M AWAKE NOW. BUT I'VE DECIDED WE'RE *NOT* BREAKING OUT NEXT WEEK.

YOU'VE *CANCELLED* THE ESCAPE?

NOT AT ALL, BUT WE'RE NOT GOING TO GIVE THE BAD GUYS A CHANCE TO SPOT OUR PREPARATIONS.

WE'RE NOT ESCAPING NEXT WEEK, WE'RE GOING TONIGHT. RIGHT *NOW.*

HAND ME MY PANTS!

NEXT: I LEAD THE GREAT ESCAPE, KILL MR. REVISE, SEDUCE PRIS AND HER TWO HOT SISTERS, DUMP GOLDIE AND FIND A WONDERFUL TREASURE. THEN IN THE SECOND HALF OF THE BOOK...

:HUFF!: :HUFF!: :HUFF!: :HUFF!:

FINALLY!

HELLO? *HELLO?*

SOMEONE'S IN TROUBLE AT THE OLD OAK!

HELLO?!

AW, *DAMMIT.*

JACKRABBIT

"YOU FLY UP TO THE GUARD TOWERS AND GET THEIR ATTENTION. MAKE SURE THEY SEE YOU.

HELLO, BOYS! FANCY A GOOD TIME?

THAT'S SUICIDE, JACK! THEY HAVE *DOUBLING ROOKS* IN THOSE TOWERS!

ONCE WE TAKE TO THE SKY, THEY'LL BE ON US IN A *HEARTBEAT.*

"I'M WELL AWARE OF THAT. IN FACT, I'M *COUNTING* ON IT."

DEPLOY THE ROOK!

I'M ON IT.

LIVE ANIMAL

"SO WE MAKE SURE THEY HAVE PLENTY OF MUNDY BIRDS TO EAT, DRAWN IN FROM OUTSIDE THE VILLAGE.

THEN WHAT HAPPENS?

THEN, WITH ANY LUCK...

"...THINGS GET HECTIC."

FAIRIES, GO TO GROUND!

WHAT'S *THAT* SUPPOSED TO MEAN?

THE DOUBLING ROOKS. THEY'RE USING THEM FOR COVER.

THIS IS *NO* AIR ESCAPE.

HVUV-VUV-HVUH

REVISE AND HIS FUCKING SECRET OPERATIVES. DOES ANYBODY KNOW *ANYTHING* AROUND HERE?

LISTEN, TAKE WHAT BAGMEN YOU NEED AND GET MOBILE.

IF THESE FABLES AREN'T *MORONS,* SOME OF THEM WILL SUCCESSFULLY MAKE IT OVER THE FENCE TONIGHT. I'LL STOP AS MANY AS I CAN.

THEY'RE READY. BUT SHOULDN'T...

YES?

...SHOULDN'T SOMEONE WAKE THE HEAD LIBRARIAN?

REVISE DOESN'T *SLEEP,* HONEY. HE ALREADY KNOWS HOW *DEARLY* WE'VE SCREWED UP HERE.

AND IF YOU VALUE YOUR LIFE--

--I WOULDN'T GO ANYWHERE *NEAR* HIM RIGHT NOW.

BECAUSE THE SKY'S TOO **FULL** OF OUR OWN GODDAMN AIR-PIRANHA, **THAT'S** WHY!

WHICH SHOULDN'T BE POSSIBLE, SINCE THEY KEEP DOUBLING ONLY AS LONG AS THE FOOD SUPPLY HOLDS OUT.

HOW MANY AIRBORNE ESCAPEES CAN THERE **BE?**

NONE.

OUR CURRENT INFORMATION IS THE PRISONERS SOMEHOW ATTRACTED THOUSANDS OF MUNDY BIRDS IN FROM THE OUTSIDE.

THAT'S WHAT THE ROOKS ARE FEEDING ON, WHICH THEY'LL **KEEP** DOING, BECAUSE WE'RE IN THE MIDDLE OF THE GODDAMN IDAHO FOREST WILDERNESS.

HOW MANY MUNDY BIRDS INHABIT THIS REGION? MILLIONS?

BILLIONS?

WE'VE NEVER ANTICIPATED THIS SCENARIO IN ANY OF OUR TRAINING DOCTRINES.

YOU'VE ALMOST GOT TO **ADMIRE** THE FABLES. FOR ONCE THEY'VE CONCOCTED A PRETTY IMPRESSIVE ESCAPE PLAN.

WE DON'T HAVE TO ADMIRE **ANYONE,** ASSISTANT LIBRARIAN BANDERHOVEN!

EXCEPT PEOPLE WHO DON'T LET **GOSSIP** INTERRUPT THEIR WORK!

YES, MISS PAGE. SORRY, MA'AM. WON'T HAPPEN AGAIN.

TIGER!!

YAP! YAP! YA--*URK!*

OH DEAR!

TOTO!

LEAVE HIM!

IT MAY SOUND HARSH, BUT I'M KIND OF *RELIEVED.*

THAT'S THE FIRST TIME THAT FLEA-BITTEN MONGREL'S QUIT YAPPING IN A HUNDRED YEARS!

90

I VOTE WE MAKE HASTE TO REMOVE OURSELVES FROM THIS COMFORTABLE, BUT ULTIMATELY *INADEQUATE* RETIREMENT VILLAGE, MR. CARPENTER.

I CONCUR MOST *HEARTILY*, MR. WALRUS.

WAIT!

GUYS!

WE'RE!

COMING!

TOO!

GREAT! JUST *GREAT!* THE ENTIRE CAMP IS MAKING A BREAK, AND *I* GET STUCK WITH CLAM RETRIEVAL.

MAKE ONE DRUNKEN *PASS* AT ROBIN PAGE DURING ONE LOUSY OFFICE PARTY AND GET STUCK WITH THE SHIT DETAILS FOR *LIFE...*

WHA-HOOOO!

MISS PAGE, WOULD YOU LIKE TO EXPLAIN TO ME *WHY* TWO ESCAPING FABLES WERE KILLED BY YOUR BAGMAN?

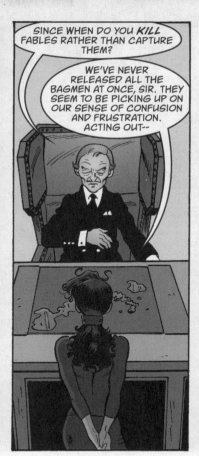

SINCE WHEN DO YOU *KILL* FABLES RATHER THAN CAPTURE THEM?

WE'VE NEVER RELEASED ALL THE BAGMEN AT ONCE, SIR. THEY SEEM TO BE PICKING UP ON OUR SENSE OF CONFUSION AND FRUSTRATION. ACTING OUT--

NOT JUST THE BAGMEN. LOOK AT *THIS*, MISS PAGE.

THIS USED TO BE *TOTO* BEFORE ONE OF YOUR SISTER'S TIGERS GOT TO IT.

I HAVE NO EXPLANATION, MR. REVISE. ROBIN TRAINS THEM SO WELL.

WE ARE IN THE BUSINESS OF CAPTURING AND CONTAINING FABLES, NOT *KILLING* THEM. WE KEEP THEM IN CUSTODY UNTIL THE WORLD *FORGETS* THEM AND THEY LOSE ALL MAGIC.

DO YOU RECALL *WHY* WE DON'T KILL FABLES, MISS PAGE?

BECAUSE KILLED FABLES OFTEN GET MAGICALLY REPLACED BY NEW VERSIONS OF THE SAME FABLE, PERHAPS SHOWING UP IN PLACES WE CAN'T GET TO THEM.

SO YOU HAVEN'T FORGOTTEN OUR MOST *BASIC* DOCTRINE?

GOOD. I'LL TAKE THAT INTO ACCOUNT WHEN I REEVALUATE YOUR *PLACE* IN MY ORGANIZATION.

MR. TORTOISE, DID YOU KNOW THERE'S A MASS ESCAPE IN PROGRESS?

WHY NO, MR. HARE, I SEEM TO HAVE MISSED THAT SAUCY BIT OF NEWS.

PERHAPS, MR. TORTOISE, BECAUSE THERE ARE SO FEW FABLES REMAINING BEHIND TO **SPREAD** SUCH DELIGHTFUL TIDINGS?

WHY YES, MR. HARE, THAT SEEMS AS REASONABLE AN EXPLANATION FOR MY CURRENT AND ALL-TOO-EMBARRASSING UN-INFORMED CONDITION AS WE'RE LIKELY TO CONSIDER.

NOW, HAVING BEEN DULY INFORMED, WOULD YOU CARE TO **JOIN** ME IN A DASH FOR FREEDOM, MR. TORTOISE?

WHY YES, MR. HARE, I DO BELIEVE THAT WOULD **SUIT** ME.

THEN LET'S BE OFF, MR. TORTOISE!

RIGHT BEHIND YOU, MR. HARE.

RIGHT BEHIND YOU.

94

WAS THERE EVER ANY DOUBT THAT I'M THE *GREATEST* FABLE WHO EVER LIVED?

OKAY, *THIS* TIME WE'RE GETTING HIM TO THE TOP!

EVERYONE TOGETHER NOW!

ONE,... TWO...THREE... *HEAVE!*

ACCORDING TO MR. SNOOTY-PANTS, IN HIS ARROGANT SNOOTY-PANTS VOICE, NO ONE'S EVER ESCAPED FROM HIS PRECIOUS LITTLE VILLAGE.

DIDN'T YOU SAY YOU GOT TO THE TOP OF THE FENCE ON YOUR *OWN* DURING YOUR LAST ESCAPE ATTEMPT?

YEAH, BUT THAT TIME I HAD A *TIGER* CHASING ME.

I'M HERE JUST A FEW WEEKS AND THE WHOLE CAMP IS IN CHAOS AND EVERYONE'S GETTING AWAY.

YEAH, I COULD SEE WHERE THAT WOULD BE A MOTIVATOR.

ONE,... TWO...THREE... *HEAVE!*

NO ONE BUT ME COULD PULL OFF THIS CAPER. I'M SO GREAT, SOMETIMES I EVEN DAZZLE MYSELF.

WHOA!

OKAY, CAREFUL NOW! YOU DON'T WANT TO *FALL* FROM UP HERE, MR. D.

NOW YOU NEED TO BALANCE ON YOUR OWN FOR A SECOND, WHILE WE GET DOWN TO CATCH YOU ON THE OTHER SIDE.

ONE REGRET, THOUGH.

I'M SURPRISED AT YOU, GOLDIE. YOU'RE ALMOST BEING *NICE* TO OUR MAN HUMPTY.

WHOA!

WHY NOT? EGG-BASED LIFE IS AS LEGITIMATE AS OURS. ACTING AS IF ONE IS INHERENTLY SUPERIOR TO THE OTHER IS OPPRESSOR BEHAVIOR.

I'M LEAVING HERE BEFORE I COULD NAIL ALL THREE PAGE SISTERS IN OLD MAN REVISE'S PRIVATE HOT TUB.

SEE THAT, MR. D? AS LONG AS GOLDILOCKS INCLUDES YOU IN HER REVO-LUTIONARY CAUSES, YOU'RE OKAY IN HER BOOK.

WHOA!

OKAY NOW, TRY TO LET YOURSELF DOWN EASY.

IT'S SO OBVIOUS ALL THREE OF THE PAGES WANT ME-- EVEN THE ONE WHO HASN'T MET ME YET.

IT'S JUST EVERYONE *ELSE* SHE TREATS LIKE SOME-THING SHE FOUND ON THE BOTTOM OF HER SHOE.

KEEP TALKING THAT WAY, JACK, AND I'LL *REMEMBER* IT, COME THE REVOLUTION.

EASY NOW--WE'LL CATCH YOU.

THEY'LL JUST HAVE TO WORK A BIT HARDER TO EVENTUALLY GET TOGETHER WITH YOURS TRULY.

IF IT WORKS OUT AS WELL AS YOUR *LAST* REVOLUTION, I'M SAFE ENOUGH.

OH, NO! JACK! THERE'S A *BAGMAN* COMING!

HUH?

OKAY, THIS ISN'T GOING AT ALL LIKE I EXPECTED.

FOR BEING FULL OF NOTHING, THIS THING IS FAR TOO STRONG.

NOT GOOD AT ALL, JACK.

:ACK!:

HEY!

WHAT ARE YOU *DOING*, SAM?

GOT TO SAVE THAT BOY BEFORE THE THING *STRANGLES* HIM.

IN A SECOND HE'LL BE OUT COLD, AND IN A DOZEN MORE HE'LL BE *DEAD*.

AND WHAT CAN *YOU* DO?

I GOT A NOTION I'VE BEEN WANTING TO TEST.

NOW SEEMS LIKE THE TIME TO TRY IT.

CLICK

GET *OFFA'* THAT BOY, YOU BIG BAG OF *NO-GOOD!*

YOW!

UGGH!

OKAY, OLD MAN. *IGNORE* THE PAIN. IGNORE THE MONSTER RUNNING FAST AT YOU.

JUST REMEMBER WHERE THE *KNIFE* LANDED.

TOO
LATE!

⸘YERK!⸘

BREATHING'S HARD, RASPY AND IT HURTS. I CAN'T SEE VERY WELL YET.

BUT THE BLURRY BLOB IN FRONT OF ME LOOKS LIKE IT MAY BE THE **BAD** GUY.

HANG ON, JACK! HANG ON, JACK! HANG **ON**, JACK!

RIDE THIS BUCKING BAG OF ASS!

HOLD ON!

HERE I COME!

GOT YOU NOW!

OH DEAR.

WHATEVER'S HAPPENING TO THAT THING, I HOPE IT *HURTS*. A LOT.

BUT THE THING THAT'S INSIDE OF THE DEFLATED BAGMAN ISN'T SOMETHING THAT SHOULD EVER BE SEEN--NOT OUTSIDE OF THE DEEPEST PIT IN HELL.

AND IT SCREAMS SOMETHING THAT ISN'T QUITE A SOUND, BUT MAKES MY BONES *SHIVER* IN A VERY NON-METAPHORICAL WAY.

IN THE DISTANT BACKGROUND I'M VAGUELY AWARE OF SAM SOBBING OUT A PLEA FOR IT TO PLEASE, IN THE NAME OF GOD, GO AWAY.

THEN AGAIN, IT MIGHT HAVE BEEN ME.

AFTER SCREAMING ITS RAGE FOR A WHILE, THE PHANTOM THING LEAVES-- FLYING BACK TOWARDS THE GOLDEN BOUGHS.

THAT WAS SOMETHING, HUH?

SHUT UP, GOLDIE.

UH-OH. GUYS?

THE TIGERS HAVE FOUND US!

ONE DAMNED THING AFTER ANOTHER! STILL GOT YOUR KNIFE, SAM?

NO! STAY *BACK!* THIS ROUND IS MINE!

YOU'RE ABOUT TO SEE WHAT AN OLD *CANNON* FROM COLCHESTER CAN DO.

I DON'T DO *THAT* VERY OFTEN, AND NEVER RECENTLY BECAUSE EGGSHELL ISN'T AS TOUGH AS FORGED STEEL, YOU KNOW.

I WAS AFRAID I MIGHT--

DAMN! I WAS AFRAID *THIS* MIGHT HAPPEN!

NO!

COME ON, JACK. MR. D'S DONE FOR, BUT *WE* CAN STILL ESCAPE IF WE KEEP GOING.

NOT YET.

MORE OF MISS PAGE'S TIGERS.

WHAT DO WE DO NOW?

STAY STILL. THEY'LL GO AFTER THE FIRST ONE WHO RUNS.

SO I'LL GIVE THEM SOMETHING TO *CHASE*.

THIS ISN'T POSSIBLE.

STAND *ASIDE*, MISS PAGE. LET ME TEST--

--BUTTER?

SAM!

HE WAS ONE OF MY GREATEST SUCCESSES.

I HAD HIM NEUTERED. *DEADENED.*

HIS STORY WAS OVER--CENSORED, SHUNNED AND FORGOTTEN BY THE OVERSENSITIVE MUNDYS.

THIS IS MORE OF JACK'S INFLUENCE. HE'S CORRUPTED *EVERYTHING* IN THE VILLAGE.

OH, HOW HE'LL BE MADE TO PAY. IT'S THE MEMORY HOLE FOR *HIM.*

HERE IT IS.

THIS WELL BELONGED TO THE FARM THAT WAS HERE BEFORE REVISE AND HIS CREW MOVED IN. IT'S BEEN MODIFIED, THOUGH.

NOW IT'S ONE OF THEIR SECRET ESCAPE ROUTES IN *CASE* THEY'RE DISCOVERED. A TUNNEL AT THE BOTTOM LEADS AWAY TO--

AND *HOW* EXACTLY DO YOU KNOW ALL THIS, GOLDIE?

I ALLOWED THE MALE GUARDS TO OBJECTIFY ME SEXUALLY IN RETURN FOR INFORMATION.

THAT SEEMS TO BE A TIME-HONORED *TECHNIQUE* WITH YOU.

IF YOU THINK I'M GOING DOWN THERE, YOU'RE CRAZIER THAN YOU LOOK, SWEETHEART.

I KNOW YOU'VE BEEN COLLABORATING WITH REVISE ALL ALONG.

ARE YOU SUFFERING FROM MENTAL ILLNESS? WHAT ON *EARTH* MAKES YOU THINK THAT?

THESE.

MY GLASSES? WHAT DO *THEY* HAVE TO DO WITH--

YOU THINK I'M AN IDIOT? ALL OF REVISE'S PEOPLE WEAR THEM. *EVERY* SINGLE ONE.

OH. MY. GODDESS.

SO YOU CAN RUN BACK AND TELL YOUR PAL REVISE THAT I'M NOT QUITE AS *THICK* AS THE REST.

YOU'RE RIGHT, JACK.

YOU'RE MUCH, *MUCH* THICKER.

I WEAR GLASSES BECAUSE *I HAVE BAD EYE-SIGHT!*

OKAY, WHATEVER. THE POINT IS, I'M NOT GOING DOWN ANY DARK HOLES ON YOUR SAY-SO. YOU HAVE FUN, THOUGH.

BELIEVE ME, JACK--I FULLY *INTEND* TO.

CHK-CHIK

SORRY, BABE. I DIDN'T COME THIS *FAR* TO GET THROWN DOWN A WELL.

IT DOESN'T SOUND LIKE A WHOLE HELL OF A LOT OF FUN, TO BE HONEST WITH YOU.

BUT I'LL LET *YOU* BE THE JUDGE.

NOOOOOO!

WOMEN!

THIS WAY, SIR. THE WELL.

SOMEONE'S DOWN THERE, SIR. I'LL HAVE SOMEONE BRING AROUND ONE OF THE JEEPS WITH A WINCH.

NO. I HAVEN'T TIME FOR THAT.

LET'S GET THIS OVER WITH.

GOT HER!

ROBIN AND PRISCILLA, MAY I PRESENT.... ....MY INFORMANT.

GET UP.

IT WAS JACK. HE TRICKED ME.

DON'T PLAY GAMES WITH ME, LITTLE GIRL.

YOU KNEW THE PLAN. YOU KNEW YOUR PART. THIS WAS TO HAVE BEEN A SIMPLE EXERCISE, TO DETERMINE WHO AMONG THEM WAS OF A MIND TO FLEE.

INSTEAD, DOZENS HAVE ACTUALLY ESCAPED. OTHERS WERE KILLED AND WILL POSSIBLY BE RECREATED ELSEWHERE, OUT OF OUR REACH.

AND I COME TO FIND MY PRIZE INFORMANT MILES AWAY FROM HER APPOINTED STATION, HEAD FIRST DOWN AN OLD WELL.

I'M SORRY, SIR. JACK FIGURED OUT I WAS WORKING FOR YOU, BUT FOR A COMPLETELY STUPID REASON.

I'VE PULLED YOU OUT OF THE WATER TWICE NOW, GOLDILOCKS.

NEXT TIME I WON'T BOTHER.

MAYBE SOME TIME IN THE MEMORY HOLE WILL DO YOU GOOD.

Jack
Pass ONE

Tony Akins
2005

Jack
Pass THREE

Tony Akins
2005

Mr. Revise
PossONE

TonyAkins 2005

Humpty Dumpty
per 1648 Royalist
attire.

Tony Akins

Goldielocks
Pass ONE

digtle braids

Tony Atkins
2005